Simon Says

*Principles and Perspectives from
Dr. Simon V. Anderson*

Elliott J. Anderson

Copyright © 2020 Elliott J. Anderson

Published by Clifton Hills Press, Valparaiso, Indiana

All rights reserved, including the right to reproduce this book or portions thereof in any form whatsoever. For information, please contact us at:
         Clifton Hills Press
         386 Deer Ridge Road
         Valparaiso, Indiana 46385

Edited by Dr. Warren J. Anderson

Cover art and layout by Tim May

Printed in the United States of America

ISBN-13: 978-0-915725-20-5

Engagement picture from 1958

Dedication

Simon Says is dedicated to Simon's wife, and my mother, Nancy. Simon was quick to tell everybody the smartest decision he ever made was marrying Nancy. This was more than a positive affirmation and encouragement often rendered in her presence. This was a recognition and proclamation of Simon's need and love for her at a soul level. He understood her profound contribution to the fulfillment of his dreams and aspirations. Their partnership was complementary and consistent. Simon needed to lead and be in control of his environment; Nancy needed to be led and was willing to release control to him. Simon needed a woman of faith and commitment; Nancy needed a man of strength and security. Simon was organized but also random and spontaneous; Nancy is also organized but also linear and structured. Simon was introverted but social; Nancy is extraverted but also enjoys time alone. They both were passionate about education and family. They both were driven to escape poverty and to create new legacies.

Nancy was the perfect counterbalance to Simon in our home and upbringing. Because my father's schedule was jammed to capacity with teaching, speaking, performing, directing, and conducting, we needed our mother's consistent structure and processing to stabilize the home. She is extremely consistent in communication and character. You can count on her for rock-solid faith and comfortingly predictable practices. This allowed us to use her as a foundational framework for our passions, drives, and movements. It allowed us to pursue our dreams and to follow our father in energy, performance, and achievement. She loved to provide food and our home for our friends. She loved to watch our games and performances and to celebrate our victories and our successes like the cheerleader she had been in her past. She held high standards and high expectations for us, centered around our commitment to the Lord and doing our best in all circumstances.

There is no Dr. Simon V. Anderson, as we knew him, without Nancy Patricia Coon becoming Nancy Anderson. It's not that he wouldn't have done some great things in music and performance had he never met her, but his legacy as a supreme educator, a community influencer, an advocate for cultural diversity, an inspiring church choir director, a dedicated family man, and a fantastic father would not have happened in anywhere near the same capacity without Mom by his side, in his corner, anchoring his ship, and securing his soul. The Lord said when he created man in Genesis 2 that it was not good for man to be alone. And for Simon, the moment he met Nancy, he was never alone again. We are all the benefactors of this union. *Simon Says* would not have even been a concept without her.

Simon Says is dedicated to Nancy Anderson, the one who infused Simon with the love of Jesus and the love of her heart, mind, and soul for 60 years.

Joyful couple, summer of 1989

Church directory 2000

Introduction

My father, Dr. Simon V. Anderson, was a small man in stature but a large man in impact and influence. Many of you had him in class, sang in his choir, rode in one of his station wagons, or worked with him at the University of Cincinnati. He lived a long and prosperous life, succumbing to vascular dementia in 2016. His passing brought many letters, emails, and phone calls to our family, with many sharing how Simon had influenced and inspired your lives. At his funeral services, my siblings and I gave testimony to that influence in our lives and in the community. He was a great teacher and a great father. This spawned the idea to incorporate both the community and the family into a book that shared part of his story, nuggets of his inspirational teaching, and his role as our father and a father figure to many.

A part of Simon's story is his poor and difficult childhood. Some of the memories may trigger strong emotions for those of you who have experienced similar challenges. Another part of his story is his faith in Jesus Christ as his Lord and Savior and his 40+ years leading music ministries in churches. This book is not an evangelistic effort, but it does give appropriate space for the place faith in God had in Simon's life and in the life of our family. Because Simon dedicated his entire professional career to teaching, as did my mother, this book is also educational. Following every chapter there are questions and exercises for reflection and introspection. Consider it your homework from Simon. Not surprisingly, education is the family business; all three of his children, a daughter-in-law, and two grandchildren also work in schools.

The ten chapters are based on sayings that Simon repeated to the point of iconic dogma. Some of these phrases he used publicly and were heard in his classes or with his choirs regularly. Some of them were just used at home for the family. I believe you will easily identify and understand the intention behind these phrases and, if desired, be able to assimilate them into your own life. There was nothing Simon enjoyed more than helping someone find their true self through music, their passion, their inspiration, their future—i.e., "why the Good Lord put them on the earth." Though he was not aware of this book project prior to his death, he would be thrilled if his sayings produced growth and development in any of his former students, colleagues, choir members, or friends. He'd also be thrilled if there were people who did not know him who were inspired by his story and his message.

I hope *Simon Says* inspires you to be your best. Make it happen!

Rev. Elliott J. Anderson
Simon's middle child and second son

Proverbs 4:20-21: *"My son, give attention to my words; incline your ear to my sayings. Do not let them depart from your sight; keep them in the midst of your heart."*

Cincinnati College-Conservatory of Music Office 1990's

Table of Contents

Chapter 1	*"Get Happy"* Attitude and Perspective	1
Chapter 2	*"Fix It"* Focus and Will	17
Chapter 3	*"Make it Happen"* Determination and Drive	29
Chapter 4	*"Watch Close Small Bear"* Mentoring and Modeling	43
Chapter 5	*"Sparkle and Shine"* Performance and Presentation	55

| Chapter 6 | *"Smile When You Say that Slim"* | 71 |
| | Discipline and Authority | |

| Chapter 7 | *"Bravo!"* | 83 |
| | Encouragement and Belief | |

| Chapter 8 | *"In the House of the Lord"* | 95 |
| | Faith and Family | |

| Chapter 9 | *"Rucka Chucka, Rucka Chucka"* | 109 |
| | Rhythm and Responsibility | |

| Chapter 10 | *"Glad to be Here"* | 121 |
| | Joy and Passion | |

About the Author	135
For More Information	137

Wedding Day, June 14, 1958

Chapter 1
"Get Happy"
Attitude and Perspective

My father was a music sociologist. His love of music was pure and passionate. He loved to listen, to compose, to analyze, to create, and to perform. But it was music's impact on society, community, and people that excited him even more. This two-pronged approach was true for our family also. He loved having a wife and children and enjoyed our chaotic cohesiveness, but our family wasn't just for us. He wanted us to have an impact in our communities, on our teams, and with our bands, friends, or groups. Perhaps the greatest attribute our family possessed through his leadership was our attitude and perspective on life, summarized by one of Simon's favorite sayings, "Get happy!"

Though the phrase "Get happy!" sounds trite and simplistic, if not based in denial, it actually is physiologically and psychologically sound. Research has shown our attitude and perspective on life makes a tremendous difference in our ability to manage and navigate our circumstances, and finding the silver lining behind every cloud is, in reality, an excellent way to handle obstacles and setbacks. Simon used the phrase most often when one of his three children sulked, complained, or responded to life in a way that was negative, pessimistic, or hopeless. He tolerated very little whining and accepted very few excuses; by the time you received the "Get happy!" mandate, you had already used your fill of both.

"Get Happy"

Some psychologists (don't count my sister or me in this group) believe "Get happy!" is actually dangerous for a young person to hear—that this mandate to change your attitude and perspective regardless of your emotions, feelings, or pain can create false identities or inauthentic coping mechanisms. Some of this might be true, but that was not my father's point. Simon didn't ask us to deny our feelings or to ignore real pain or suffering; rather, he told us to choose how we would respond to it. We had to recognize it. We had to accept it. We had to find a way to be happy regardless of whatever happened. He didn't want a fake happiness with no real introspection or analysis but an authentic response to the moment and a joy for life, and even an appreciation for the experience, that went beyond our circumstances. We are blessed and we should act that way.

"Get happy!" played out for me the most in my athletics. My father preferred I allow the fire of my intensity to spill out on occasion rather than refrain from taking charge or leading. He would constantly tell me I was the best player on the floor, field, or court, so "act like it!" He didn't mean that in a selfish way. I was a good teammate, and you can't lead your team if you act as if you are above them. But he also told me I had a responsibility to the team, to perform at my best at all times and to play with intensity, determination, and the will to win. In grade school and middle school, this often led to post-game tantrums or meltdowns, and he allowed me those moments before redirecting my passion. By high school, my athletic demeanor was stoic, but the fire inside remained, and my ability to manage the game's emotion was secure. I played like my dad taught, with passion, persistence, and intensity. The end goal and the result were always in mind, but I could adapt and move with the spirit of the moment. I chose to lead. I chose to love. I chose to play with passion and joy no matter what.

The "Get happy!" theme appears frequently in Karin's writing and podcasts. This isn't surprising because she probably received the mandate from our father the most. She was a female and the baby in the family. These two distinctions would often move her toward emotional responses. Karin wasn't prone to overly emotional sensitivity or rashly immature responses, but our father was quick to correct improper attitude or perspective no matter how rare or infrequent. As an adult, Karin is still wonderfully emotional and passionate; her decision to be happy, positive, and blessed has not suppressed any of her feelings or emotions. In fact, "Get happy!" has sharpened her feelings, defined her emotions, and impacted her followers who respond via her classes, lectures, books, and messages.

The reality, of course, is life is not easy. Life is hard. There are plenty of reasons to be unhappy, discouraged, or depressed. We all face physical, mental, emotional, and spiritual challenges that can be overwhelming. Simon wouldn't tell you to pretend these difficult things weren't happening. He would challenge you to overcome them, to move through and beyond them, to read positive books, listen to your favorite music, engage in your favorite activities, and connect with the positive and joyful people in your life. If you couldn't get happy yourself, then you better find the people in your life who could help you get happy and join them.

The irony of this message for Simon was he fought many insecurities and fears and rarely reached out to others for happiness. (As an introvert, he preferred to be alone to alter his mood, and it always involved music. You could tell what mood he was in by what music he listened to or played—jazz when he was happy, classical when he was contemplative, country when he was sad, choral and church music when he was focused, rock or rap was when he was edgy.) That's probably why his message about attitude and perspective was so passionate and persistent. As a father he gave us the security and confidence he was not given when he was young. People often asked me why my father did so many things, why he worked so hard with so many jobs, why he always was writing, researching, teaching, and performing. (He slept very little at night and took cat naps during the day.) As I grew older, I realized he had to live that way to overcome the negativity, abuse, and shaming of his family of origin. That was his way to choose a positive and happy path that provided for his family and kept him in community, impacting and influencing others, even though he was so private. The hardest two weeks of his year probably occurred during our annual family summer vacation. We always had fun when we visited our parents' families in Wisconsin, but without the routine of all his work, he would lose his focus and his drive. That's why every vacation included writing or composing a new work to help fill the gap in structure and pace. To my dad, work was relaxing and vacation wasn't, and visiting the environment where so much pain occurred didn't help him either.

My mother did not have an easy upbringing either. Her father died when she was two. Her older brother had to drop out of school to help on the farm. Her mother remarried, which brought a significant change in her environment, and she battled through an eating disorder. After she married my father, the two of them were poor and ambitious, but through a ton of hard work, belief, and faith, they built a beautiful life of consistent joy and purpose. Work stabilized their marriage; their work ethics were uncompromising. My mother never missed a single class in her entire academic career. When she retired from Doherty School, she had accrued almost three years of sick pay!

Two children of the early post-Depression years—with sometimes very unhappy upbringings, including death, abuse, addiction, and poverty—decided to "Get happy!" in marriage and did so for 58 years. They chose to stay committed to each other, to be great parents to their kids, and to be happy. I interviewed them in 1990 for one of my graduate-school classes on marriage and family. Both were adamant regarding what allows a marriage to survive and thrive during the challenges of life. "You committed to God and to each other. Divorce was not an option. Get happy! Make the best of it. Take the good and throw away the bad." Do you hear the message?

Those of you who had my father in class saw and heard his attitude and perspective during every lecture. We did, too. Simon parented like he taught, which sometimes included long lectures. Warren and I also took Music Appreciation with him at UC. I came home from college and took it between my freshman and sophomore year. It was fun to see his persona and spirit of leadership and life through the lens of the class syllabus and the musical genres we covered, which wasn't a lot different than listening to him around the kitchen table or on the way home from a game. Broaden your musical perspective. Experience things outside of your comfort zone. Believe in yourself and your abilities. Challenge yourself to new and greater things. Don't be afraid of or fear anything, except the Lord. Use your gifts for the community. Share your talent with the world. Give your best effort. Pursue excellence, but don't get caught up in the grade or the degree. Learn. Grow. Love. Live. Move. Believe. I know the students that have been in classes taught by Warren, Karin, and me have heard the same message.

What is your attitude about life right now? Do you need an attitude adjustment? Does your perspective on life need realignment? Choosing to be happy, positive, friendly, giving, and loving might take some time to assimilate into your daily life, but, once you do it, it will make a tremendous difference for you and for your friends, family, and co-workers. After you have incorporated the perspective of being blessed and blessing others through your attitude and communication, your relational impact will grow exponentially. And when there are moments when you are weary, worn, and run down and you inevitably

"Get Happy"

start to whine, complain, bicker, or get overly critical and negative, look in the mirror and tell yourself to "Get happy!"

Philippians 4:8: *"Finally, brothers and sisters, whatever is true, whatever is noble, whatever is right, whatever is pure, whatever is lovely, whatever is admirable—if anything is excellent or praiseworthy—think about such things and the God of peace will be with you."*

"Happiness is a decision." — **Michael J Fox**

Simon Says

First Christmas together, 1958

"Get Happy"

Simon Says:

What do you need to do to "Get happy" today?

List five things.

1._____

2._____

3._____

4._____

5._____

Whom will your choice of happiness impact the most besides you?

_____

_____

What attitudes in your life do you need to change?

_____

_____

What new perspective do you need to incorporate into your life?

_____

_____

Who are the people in your life that help you "Get happy"?

_____

_____

"Get Happy"

_____

_____

What activities in your life get you happy? Do them!

_____

_____

_____

_____

Simon Says

Anderson Family 2013

Classroom Persona 1990's

Chapter 2
"Fix It"
Focus and Will

Simon had either extreme focus or a lack of focus in life, depending on his level of interest in, his amount of passion for, or the deadline date of the subject at hand. He was the carrier of the ADHD gene that came from his father, then through me, and providentially is with my two sons, despite the lack of direct genetic influence. This Anderson ADHD gene manifests itself in significant creative and artistic energy both essential to our careers and difficult to harness or contain.

Because focus was a challenge for Simon, his "will" became the counterbalance necessary to his success. Sometimes you could watch him wrestle with his focus and will when he had limited time and multiple deadlines for the tasks at hand, often culminating in a frenetic set of random movements—fueled by a Coke, some popcorn, and a rush of heightened focus—to accomplish what needed to be done. It also usually involved staying up until 1:00 or 2:00 in the morning, though his normal morning routine would not be altered.

Since Simon had figured out what he had to do to use his will to focus and achieve, he expected us to do the same. Warren was structured, mature, organized, and responsible, so those traits became the standard operating procedures for his academic and musical life. When Warren had a moment of immaturity or irresponsibility, my father would quickly rebuke, correct, and admonish him, usually accompanied by one of his most iconic phrases. "Fix it!" was one of the

"Fix It"

statements my father only used at home. My dad had some handyman skills, but this phrase had nothing to do with construction or repairs. "Fix it!" was a mandate communicated without a smile and with significant exhortation. With flushed face and bulged-out eyes, he drove the point home with his right index finger used to accentuate his point in rhythm with the harshly aspirated consonant sound of the *F*. The word *Fix* came out with such tremendous force, volume, and enunciated clarity, it could make me run or hide, depending on which response removed me most quickly from his intensity and accountability.

For Warren and Karin, "Fix It!" was a random, once-every-other-month statement that quickly helped them return to their normal responsibility and execution that, for whatever reason, was temporarily lacking. For me, it was a weekly mantra of exasperation, a plea for compliance that sometimes included five or six options for possible fixes to whatever mess I had created. The foundational message behind "Fix it!" was a call to action, a reminder that excellence was required and an emphatic notice that laziness and undisciplined responses to life would not be tolerated or accepted as the norm. Even if your lack of ability or talent were the problem, Simon demanded that your will be activated at full focus to see if you could overcome the deficiency. Effort, energy, and commitment could compensate for many inadequacies.

The second primary focus of "Fix it!" was the urgency of the moment. "Fix it!" did not mean putting the issue on a list somewhere and working on it over the next few weeks or months. "Fix it!" meant attending to this matter immediately. "Fix it!" was often followed by "I don't care what you have to do to get this done, but I want it done right now," or words to that effect. "Fix it!" was a call to order, a call to focus, a call to urgency. It was a call to activate your will and overcome any obstacle or issue. This mandate, when in response to my academic struggles, led to some monumental battles of will between the two most competitive people in our family. Only after I was able to harness my intelligence into academic success in late college and graduate school were we able to laugh about some of the all-night battles we had about my homework. I also realize our wars of will usually focused us both; my behavioral issues kept Dad focused on his family and gave me the extra attention I needed to learn how to cope and use my gifts.

Focus is often an abstract concept in our personal lives. Focus doesn't mean simply being organized and orderly. Some really structured and detailed people lack focus in their work and might get their work done, but without joy and passion. They don't inspire or influence others for effectiveness or excellence. Focus to Simon was about knowing who you are, how you operate, and what you needed to be effective and excellent at your work, with your family, and in your community. Focus started with self-awareness and then moved into the ability to maximize your time and energy in order to accomplish your prioritized tasks and duties. Simon believed your will had to be involved in this process because you had to know your long-term goals and dreams in order to stay passionate and engaged in your routine and mundane responsibilities.

Simon also believed that if we lacked focus it might mean that we were in the wrong line of work. If our will could not actively motivate our focus in order to be successful and joyful in our vocation, then we might need to consider a different path for our provisions. Almost all of us, he would say, have plenty of focus and drive where our favorite hobbies or passions are concerned. The trick is to turn one of those hobbies or passions into a primary form of income if your current work is boring or oppressive, no matter how well it pays. My father's main passions were teaching, composing, writing, and performing, and he made sure they brought income into our family budget.

"Fix It"

When we are out of focus and our will is wandering, it is time to evaluate our circumstances, our priorities, and our convictions to make sure we have head, heart, and soul alignment. If we have incongruence between what we know is right, what we feel is right, and what we believe is right, then we will be wishy washy in our decisions and our focus will be blurred. We need to be flexible and adaptable to life's changes but also be pretty zeroed in on who we are, what we are, and how we are. I obviously have significant focus issues also. I have had about seven careers already, but I learned early in my 20's that it did not matter if I were coaching, teaching, preaching, painting, administrating, or writing—every expression and every outlet in my work was about mentoring and shepherding people toward a better understanding of their faith and themselves and their ability to impact their community for the Kingdom of God. Because I have mainly worked in Christian institutions or agencies, this has been more blatantly evangelistic than the work Simon and Nancy did in their careers, but the method of investment and engagement is the same. For many of us, we will struggle with focus and will unless we submit our will to God's will, which centers our focus on His Kingdom and His message.

Matthew 22:37: *"You shall love the Lord your God with all your heart and with all your soul and with all your mind. This is the great and first commandment."*

"Successful people maintain a positive focus in life no matter what is going on around them. They stay focused on their past successes rather than their past failures, and on the next action steps they need to take to get them closer to the fulfillment of their goals rather than all the other distractions that life presents to them."
— **Jack Canfield**

"Fix It"

Rhinelander, WI High School band, 1948

Simon Says:

Are your focus and will aligned right now?

Yes   No

If not, how come?

_____

What do you need to do to get them aligned?

_____

Are your head, heart, and soul aligned?

Yes   No

If not, how come?

_____

What do you need to do to get them aligned?

"Fix It"

Where do you have the best focus in your life?

Does this focus relate to your primary income?

       Yes   No

   If not, could it?

Have you submitted your will to God's will?

       Yes   No

   If not, would you consider it?

Dexter, Michigan High School Staff Pictures, 1959/1960

Chapter 3
"Make It Happen"
Determination and Drive

Sharon Vance Anderson, the name that appears on the birth certificate of Dr. Simon V. Anderson, was a very driven man. He grew up with a name he didn't like, so when he was old enough to change it, he did. He grew up poor and unimportant, so he vowed to make enough money to be comfortable and to make a name for himself—and he did. He grew up without encouragement or inspiration, so he determined to encourage and inspire others—and he did. When

Simon committed to a career in music education, he was driven to be one of the best music educators in the country—and he was. When Simon wanted a better music appreciation textbook, he decided to write his own and to form his own publishing company—and he did. When Simon committed to Nancy, he was determined to have a forever marriage—and they did. When Simon had three children who showed promise in different areas of academics, athletics, and the arts, he demanded that we would be just as driven as he was—and we were. Simon and Nancy made it happen.

Simon used "Make it happen" to encourage and inspire his children to take charge of our lives and fulfill our dreams. It was a rallying cry, a challenge and command given with great joy and accompanied by a big smile that exuded incredible confidence. It was often the last thing he said to me before I left the station wagon and his immediate influence before a big game. It usually included a knuckle pinch on the thigh and a ring tap on the steering wheel. I knew he loved the big games as much as I did. "Make it happen" was an order to activate the fullness of yourself and your abilities. It was a reminder that steely determination and relentless drive will override and overcome obstacles and barriers to success. "Make it happen" was Simon's life story.

Simon worked for a year after high school to save money and then attended Wisconsin's Whitewater State Teachers College to earn a degree in education. To help pay his tuition, he played piano in nightclubs, at dinner clubs, and for parties. This important income and experience as an entertainer paved the foundation for his teaching style; he would be an educator who would entertain and inspire. His first teaching job was at Potosi High School in Wisconsin where he taught English, music, and band. Despite his degree and his age, he was drafted into the Army in 1954. He was stationed in Fort Knox, KY, and his piano and clarinet proficiency enabled him to perform regularly in the officers' club. He also received a citation for composing for the 3rd Army Division and was honorably discharged in 1956.

After the Army, Simon took a job at Colby High School back in Wisconsin and taught English, math, and band and directed glee clubs and choirs. In the summer of 1957, he traveled east as a visiting student at Ohio State University for piano training, and in the fall of 1957, he made three massive commitments. First, he committed to music education as a career. He enrolled at Stevens Point College to earn a second degree, this one in music. Second, he committed to Nancy Coon, a soprano with a strong voice and a sweet spirit. They dated over the winter and were married in the summer of 1958. Third, he committed to a middleclass lifestyle fueled by music, marriage, and family. He turned down an offer to travel overseas with a band and, with the encouragement of Dr. Hugo Marple, his music professor at Point, enrolled at the University of Michigan in the fall of 1958.

While he worked on his master's and Ph.D. degrees, Nancy taught home economics at Dexter High School outside of Ann Arbor. For one semester Simon was a full-time substitute teacher, directing the choirs and band, and taught at the high school with Nancy; they even co-hosted the talent show. In hindsight, it seems it took a while for Simon to lock into music education and teaching at the college level, but along the way he pursued more opportunities for education and experiences that allowed his passions to flourish. Sometimes "making it happen" involves a journey over a decade, not a singular decision or movement that changes everything instantly. Sometimes it is both. Either way, commit to the important values and passions in your life. "Make it happen"!

When Simon's children showed drive and determination in our passion areas, Simon soon opened the floodgates of his attention, generosity, and education. Camps, lessons, tutors, books, and articles were allocated and distributed for our digestion and participation. Often these additional movements towards our potential were premature, but the push was premeditated and meant to activate the drive, and it usually did. When it came to athletics, I was driven to be the best and to compete with ferocity, so the push wasn't necessary. But with music, the primary family gift, I was much slower in determination and was afraid to fail. This led to multiple short-lived and disastrous lessons for other instruments before I stumbled into the drums. While Simon worked with Warren on piano and bass, he heard me instinctively keeping time on the basement stairs.

Within a week I was in drum lessons at the Conservatory. When my teacher reported reasonable potential in me, Simon bought me a drum set. Only a few months after my drums were in the house, he scheduled me to perform at church. (This decision, by the way, like it was for Warren and Karin when they were first placed on stage, came out of the blue, without my knowledge or anything resembling consent.) Within a year of taking lessons from a jazz drummer, I was sitting in on jobs. And within two years, I was one of Simon's regular drummers for his trios, quartets, and even the big bands he played with, and I also joined several of Warren's bands. Education, experience, opportunities, and steady pursuit of your passion—these are the building blocks of "making it happen."

Drums allowed me a place within the family musical structure and also provided regular income during my teenage years. Simon was determined I would be an excellent drummer before I was even an average one. Simon and Warren drove me in my development through band opportunities before I was driven to be a good drummer myself. They also bought me records and played recordings for me of the greatest drummers in history. By the end of high school, I played for hours by myself to Neil Peart, Stewart Copeland, and Phil Collins. By college, I wanted to be a great drummer, no other motivations needed. Sometimes the drive and determination in our life are given to us by others who see something in us that we don't yet see.

The ethos behind "make it happen" is more important than the motivational message: preparation, practice, determination, and drive will dictate your outcomes, activating your soul in the process and bringing home the desired result. Sometimes Simon said "Make it happen" so you could find the determination needed to finish a task. Sometimes he said it to ignite the focus necessary for excellent execution during an important performance or game. Sometimes he said it to challenge you to unlock the drive he knew was in your heart, even if it were temporarily inhibited. It drove him absolutely crazy that I would score high on my standardized testing but would refuse to pursue even average academic work. He knew if I applied the determination and drive I had for athletics to my academics, similar results would follow. I discovered that for myself in college.

Simon believed each individual had the potential to make whatever IT is in their life happen, and once you understood and activated the determination and drive that were needed, you could attain almost anything. What derails us from making it happen is not usually what we think. We might have very challenging circumstances, but external situations rarely block us from growth and change. No, what we believe about ourselves and our fear of failure stop us from so many accomplishments. Our propensity to worry about what other people think usually makes IT not happen.

Simon's simple rebuttal to this faulty fear of other people's thoughts and responses was, "Who cares what so and so says or thinks about you? They have enough problems of their own to worry about." Rationally, we understand that we can't control what others think about us, and we know people talk about us behind our back and often without justification. Ultimately, we recognize this is completely outside of our control, and yet we spend hours, days, weeks, and even years totally paralyzed about a decision or a move because we are worried what other people will think about it. To quote another iconic Simon phrase, this is just "foolishness." Foolishness was thoughts, words, or deeds that were silly, inappropriate, or incorrect and which served as an excuse for not making it happen. Put away the foolishness and "make it happen!"

Isaiah 60:22: *"When the time is right, I, the Lord, will make it happen."*

"Infuse your life with action. Don't wait for it to happen. Make it happen. Make your own future. Make your own hope." — **Bradley Whitford**

"Make It Happen"

U.S. Army, 1954

Simon Says:

Where do you need to make it happen right now?

_____

_____

What areas of your life are missing drive and determination?

_____

_____

What "foolishness" are you currently believing?

_____

_____

"Make It Happen"

List the 3 areas where you have natural drive and determination.

1. _____

2. _____

3. _____

List 3 ways you can begin to make it happen, activating your drive and determination.

1. _____

2. _____

3. _____

Two Music Men: Simon and Warren, 1969

Chapter 4
"Watch Closely, Small Bear"
Mentoring and Modeling

The Berenstain Bears were the main characters in a successful series of children's books and television shows that started in the 1960's. Simon would often read these books to us, enjoying the passionate but absent-minded father bear with his propensity for mistakes and accidents despite his love and commitment to his family. Papa Bear would use the phrase, "Watch closely, Small Bear" right before he mentored his cub about some type of skill or ability, which inevitably ended up a disaster, never working the way he had intended.

For Simon, however, "Watch closely, Small Bear" was not used when he was bumbling around, but rather when he was in his areas of giftedness or when he used a skillset he wanted us to learn also. Warren received the phrase when our father showed him chord progressions or composing strategies. I heard it when he showed me how to solder or how to throw a better curveball. Karin encountered it when he showed her how to drive or how to have better breath support in her solos. Simon had learned how to learn, he had an insatiable desire to learn more, and he desperately wanted his children and his students to follow in his footsteps. Watch closely, Small Bear.

One story from Warren's early years as a bass player serves as a great example. Simon was usually excellent at bringing mentees along at a pace they could handle so that they would develop confidence and not get overwhelmed. Notice that word *usually*. Simon had a last-minute cancellation for a six-piece combo gig and needed a bassist, so he decided to give his eldest son a bit of a challenge. Just as they pulled into the parking lot and began to unload the gear, Simon said to Warren, "By the way, the trombone player tonight just got off the road with the Woody Herman band." Warren went from tolerably confident to shaking in his boots by the time they reached the front door. He couldn't believe Simon would throw him in the deep end like that, running the risk that Warren would embarrass himself and, worse, embarrass Simon in the process.

Warren took his customary position to the immediate left of Simon's keyboard and uttered a quick prayer for mercy. He breathed a bit more easily, however, when Simon started calling familiar tunes Warren knew well, giving him ample time to acclimate to the group dynamics. After a while, Simon called an unfamiliar tune, and Warren began to panic. He needn't have worried, though. Throughout that entire song and for the rest of the evening (especially whenever he called for a new tune), Simon took the index finger of his left hand and hovered it over the note Warren was to play just a split second later—chord after chord after chord—allowing Warren to "fake" his efforts with success so that no one other than father and son knew how unqualified, by the world's standards, Warren was to be there. Watch closely, Small Bear, and you'll be OK.

Simon also understood that mentoring was about how you lived your life more than it was what you said or how well you taught. Reiterating this phrase over and over let us know we could follow his and our mother's basic life principles and their values, and we would find our way and our place in this world. It may sound simplistic or Pollyanna-ish, but it is true. And isn't this an enormous part of our parenting responsibility, to show our children how to live in a way that will help them navigate their own journey?

My father did not mentor in the same way his children do. Simon's offspring are holistic mentors who dive deeply into the mental, emotional, and spiritual lives of their students and mentees. Simon was from a different generation and had the personality and temperament of that era. He wasn't counselor-oriented or pastorally minded; in fact, Simon was only an average listener, and there was a shelf life to his conversation attention, so if you wanted to disclose or confess something, you better get to the point quickly. When Karin and I both went into clinical counseling work he was skeptical of our tolerance to listen to people "whine and complain" for hour upon hour. Obviously, Simon never took part in psychotherapy.

Psychological research supports the principle behind the phrase "Watch closely, Small Bear." We learn more from what someone does by how they live than we learn by their words or instruction. Mentoring is truly about modeling behavior more than it is about instructing behavior. Jesus taught His disciples this same message right before he returned to heaven when he told them "to teach others to *observe* what He [had] commanded them" (Matthew 28:20, emphasis added). In other words, it was the job of the disciples to live out the principles of faith and love that Christ taught them, their transformed lives, when observed by others, initiating conversations or conversions. Simon believed in that principle of Christ and that principle of mentoring. He was obviously a fantastic teacher and orator, but you could learn more by watching him live than by merely listening to him teach. Watch closely, Small Bear.

Simon also knew he was a role model and relished that earned position. My parents had worked extremely hard to overcome very difficult pasts, and they enjoyed modeling an effective and inspirational life. Simon also believed that we all should be role models for each other, but if your life was a mess, don't even pretend. Get your house in order and then start teaching others how you made it through. Pay close attention to what you learned about yourself, the Lord, and life—and then pass it on to others. It was part of the learning process and the educator mindset ingrained in him. "If a teacher isn't learning," he would say, "then he has no business teaching." We children observed our parents' modeling of constant reading and research, so we also read and research as primary modes of preparation and training in our areas of study.

Mentors also come in all shapes and sizes and with all types of personalities and temperaments, but the number one criterion for someone to mentor is willingness. Simon received strong mentoring from teachers and directors in his past, and he was willing to mentor and model his life for you. It actually helped him stay on course. Are you willing to live in such a way that people will follow your lead, your teaching, your message, and your life? Simon didn't often weave stories of his own history into his mentoring. In fact, many people are shocked to learn of how difficult his life was before Nancy, the University of Michigan, and the University of Cincinnati forged together a backbone of love, commitment, education, and credibility. But as a music sociologist, he would weave the stories of the composers, musicians, and entertainers into narratives of growth, change, and encouragement and apply that to your life in a way that illuminated their music and their history for your inspiration.

Simon enjoyed the admiration and appreciation of his students, and though he couldn't always remember your name, he often remembered a piece of your story, especially if it included the need to overcome, initiate change, carve a new path, or reinvent your persona or personal life. Simon didn't want to be your pastor or your counselor. He wanted to be your inspiration and your model for growth, development,

"Watch Closely, Small Bear"

and fulfillment. He also wanted you to do the same for others. Watch closely, Small Bear.

Matthew 5:16: *"In the same way, let **your light shine** before others, that they may see **your** good deeds and glorify **your** Father in heaven."*

"A mentor is someone who allows you to see the hope inside yourself." — **Oprah Winfrey**

Anderson Quartet, 2005 (We played 25 straight New Year's Eve jobs together as a family, 1983-2008)

Simon Says:

Do you have a mentor?

Yes   No

>If yes, then keep a regular schedule of connection and communication.

>If no, then search your heart and soul for an available mentor and ask to meet.

Are you a mentor?

Yes   No

>If yes, then check on the mentee regularly and consistently.

>If no, then search your heart and soul for an available mentee and ask to meet.

What are your behaviors and communication that others can model?

_____

_____

_____

What are your behaviors and communication that you need to get in order?

_____

_____

_____

Bicentennial year choir (combined choirs of the 9th Street and other Cincinnati-area American Baptist Churches)

Chapter 5
"Sparkle and Shine"
Performance and Presentation

Simon rarely wore anything but suits. Even when he mowed the yard or worked on the car, he would have his dress clothes on and would simply tuck his tie into his buttoned-up Oxford as the only noticeable alteration in attire for the activity. I didn't see him wear a pair of jeans until he was in his 70's. An off day may have produced a sweater vest, but that was about as casual as you would see him. One afternoon when

Angie and I were home visiting and remodeling their basement, Simon took me for a man-to-man meal at then-UC Bearcats' basketball coach Bob Huggins' new restaurant. I had just started my counseling career and was working with many young people from difficult backgrounds, so I asked my dad what the most significant issue in his youth had been, couching the question in professional context with hopes to coax some disclosure. I expected to hear about the abuse, the negativity, and the hard drinking of his father. I was wrong. He said quickly, "Growing up poor." He then repeated the phrase several more times and avoided my eye contact as he sipped his Lowenbrau and stared at the sports memorabilia on the wall.

There are not many pictures of Simon as a child, but the ones we have are not pleasant. His clothes are disheveled and two sizes too big. His shoes look worn and uncomfortable. He rarely smiles and always looks sad. The moment he told me growing up poor was the most significant issue of his life, his self-mandated debonair-in-dress decisions made total sense. Simon had made it out of poverty and into a very successful life, and he was wearing his new identity. A man wearing a suit has a purpose. A man wearing a suit has importance. A man wearing a suit means something to somebody. A man wearing a suit isn't poor.

Presentation was a huge issue for Dr. Anderson, and the first part of it was based on his rise out of poverty. He loved being a professor and the notoriety and authority that came with the Ph.D., the books, the articles, and the compositions. He loved having a wife and children who were also very smart. We were a part of his success story, a part of his identity-presentation of financial freedom, academic clout, and driven achievers, with the private school, the swim club, the six station wagons, the family trophy room, and the wad of cash he always had with his money clip. Simon was very generous with the presentation of his identity and the money he had worked so hard to earn. He was always eager to treat a station wagon full of teammates or friends to a Putz's, Dairy Queen, or United Dairy Farmers ice cream cone, and he had a soft spot for our friends and the students who he knew struggled financially.

Presentation, however, meant much more to Simon than just the ascent to upper middle class. Presentation was secondarily inherently linked to performance. How you presented yourself on stage or on the field or in the classroom made a difference in your performance. When I took his Music Appreciation class in the summer of 1986, I was amazed to see he rarely looked at his notes. Each class was like a separate performance about a musical era and the key players in it, complete with impersonations, recordings, and personal accompaniment. He was in command of the classroom and knew that he had something important to share with us. His passion in presenting the material made it more interesting to you than you ever thought it could be. I hated classical music until that class, but Simon made it come alive for me and I was compelled by the human-interest stories of the great composers.

Simon's oft-repeated phrase for presentation and performance was "Sparkle and shine." When we were on stage performing, whether for church, a wedding, a party, or a night club, we were to sparkle and shine. There was to be joy and freedom in your performance, starting with your presentation. We were to smile, look poised and confident, as if we belonged on stage. When my speaking career began to blossom in my thirties, I often asked him for pointers about conveying humility and authority at the same time. He gave me some specific ideas on introductions, repetitive phrases and key points, and even some dramatic gestures for certain types of audiences, but the best advice he gave me was this: "Speak at the event as if God himself had ordained you for that very moment." This became even more important for me when I became a senior pastor in a congregation with former college and seminary professors in regular attendance.

Simon had a magnetic smile. It was a part of his new identity and the exuberance he presented. One time I asked him why he smiled so warmly when holding the hands and talking with the older women at church or at a gig. "First," he said, "I paid about $7,000 for this smile and I am going to use it." His teeth had been an absolute mess until he had the money to fix them. "And second, those widows still need male attention, and I can unite them in spirit with their husbands with the hymns or songs we sing and the recognition I give their feminine sensibilities." (Yes, he talked like this all the time.) Though separated from their older Wisconsin relatives, our parents cared in this manner for numerous seniors over the years, inviting widows and older members of the church who were alone to our house every Thanksgiving and Easter. Warren and I followed this modeling with our congregations. And the home service business I started during seminary and ran for ten years specialized in attention to the seniors in our community. "Sparkle and shine" was for all people, all the time, and presenting yourself as a confident, joyful, and kind person was not just for the stage. "It should be part of the fabric of your soul," Simon would say.

Publicly, "Sparkle and shine" was most prominently used with Simon's choirs. When Dr. Anderson stepped onto the podium to direct an anthem or cantata, audiences knew they were in for a treat. He always delivered extraordinary performances; he simply wouldn't have it any other way. This emphasis on excellence was particularly impressive given that his church choirs were made up of mostly amateur singers; many members had never taken a voice lesson or ever tried to read music.

Simon's charisma drew people to the choir, and he recruited them as well. Should you happen to visit a church where Simon was the director, you'd likely be greeted after the service with that magnetic smile, his warm handshake, and something along the lines of

"With that rich, resonant tone, you must be a singer! We could use some more voices in the men's section!" Within a week or two, you'd found a new church home and a spot in the choir loft alongside a band of baritone brothers!

Choir members adored and revered Simon. Honored to sing under the direction of such an esteemed musician, they strove to please him—which was a tall order. Not only did he expect technical precision, he also demanded enthusiasm, passion, and heart. If, in rehearsal, a number felt flat, he'd cajole the troops, "Sparkle! Sparkle! Shine! Shine!" He modeled this mandate, stomping loudly to the beat and dancing on the podium (so energetically, in fact, that at Ninth Street Baptist Church, the congregation insisted his podium be outfitted with a rail to ensure he didn't tumble off mid-anthem!) Choir members worked hard, and, in return, Simon propelled his amateurs to sparkling, shining heights they'd never believed possible. He had seen how sparkling and shining had

"Sparkle and Shine"

helped change the entire course of his own life, and he felt honored and privileged to bring just a bit of that life-changing enthusiasm to anyone who ever sat in his classrooms, lecture halls, and choir lofts, everyone who encountered his teaching, music-making, or off-the-cuff philosophizing: a lifetime of students, choirs, lecture audiences, and, especially children.

As Simon's only daughter, Karin perhaps felt the expectation to "Sparkle and shine" most keenly. Dad's infectious charisma invited—or rather, compelled—his kids to *Shoot for the stars! Make it happen! You're an Anderson!* But naturally, as children, we each went through "phases" (Mom and Dad labeled any behavior or disposition they didn't care for as a "phase." Their firm belief in the power of language assumed if they could deem the nuisance temporary, it would, in fact, pass.)

Karin recalls the tension of insecure adolescent moments juxtaposed against Dad's "sparkle and shine" mandate. Like most teens, she felt self-conscious and uncertain at times. She so admired Dad's upbeat spirit, positive temperament, and steady confidence and knew these qualities were in her DNA, but sometimes wondered if she could live up to the bar our Dad set.

But frankly, Simon didn't give his kids the chance to doubt themselves for too long. When we didn't *feel* capable, confident, or charismatic, he spoke these qualities into us. He believed we could sparkle and shine, even when we weren't so certain ourselves.

One of Karin's cherished teenage memories perfectly exemplifies this. Like most girls, she spent hours primping for a special event, dance, or prom; she'd select the right dress, get her hair "just so," and perfect her makeup. Once she put her look together, Dad would exclaim with pride, "Nancy! Get over here! There's a Hollywood star in the house—a ravishing beauty!" As a self-conscious 15-year-old, Karin didn't always *feel* self-assured in that moment. But armed with her Dad's adoration and firm belief in her sparkle, she stepped into the evening shining brightly.

Simon stoked the sparkle in his children, students, choir members, band mates, and friends. We all today shine more brightly because of his abundant, unwavering belief in us and his boundless encouragement that we share our light with the world.

Luke 2:8-10: *"And there were shepherds living out in the fields nearby, keeping watch over their flocks at night. An angel of the Lord appeared to them, and the glory of the Lord shone around them, and they were terrified. But the angel said to them, 'Do not be afraid. I bring you good news that will cause great joy for all the people.'"*

"Never forget the essence of your spark."
— **Taylor Swift**

Simon Says

Simon fixing Karin's bow, Prom 1988

"Sparkle and Shine"

Simon Says:

Who have been agents of sparkle and shine in your life?

_____

_____

_____

_____

_____

<u>Are you sparkling and shining right now?</u>

     Yes   No

     If yes, what things motivate that sparkle and shine?

If no, what steps can you take to rekindle that spark and that shine?

_____

_____

_____

_____

_____

Who needs you to be an agent of sparkle and shine in their life?

_____

_____

"Sparkle and Shine"

_____

_____

_____

_____

Simon (with his dog Penny) and his younger brother Jack, 1939

Chapter 6
"Smile When You Say That, Slim"
Discipline and Authority

My grandfather, John Anderson, came from a large Norwegian family that moved to Rhinelander, Wisconsin, from Oslo, Norway, in the early 20th century. Grandpa was smart, but he only finished the eighth grade, dropping out, as many did then, to work to help the family. Grandpa was tall and athletic and was the ace pitcher of the Rhinelander Paper Mill's summer baseball team. And Grandpa John was the original music man of the family. Like my father, he could play many instruments and played in jazz trios and quartets his whole adult life. When he lost his carpentry business in the Depression, however, his drinking escalated, his sarcasm became acidic, and his belief in God and the American Dream evaporated. He became an even stronger influence on my dad's life at this point, but not for positive reasons.

The Attention Deficit Hyperactivity Disorder (ADHD) lineage came through Grandpa John to Simon and then to me. Both John and Simon used music as the primary outlet for their energy and both men were gifted entertainers and showmen. People with ADHD can be extremely productive when busy and engaged, but that energy can become a typhoon or terror if it is not used for productivity and purpose. Grandpa John was both proud and jealous of his gifted musician son. He taught him to play, trained him to perform, and gave him early opportunities to sing and join him in clubs (just like my dad did for us), but he also condemned, criticized, and cut down Simon, often ridiculing him publicly and humiliating him privately for various real and imagined indiscretions.

Simon did not talk very often about his father or tell us about the abusive elements of the discipline he received. One of the few stories he told me stands in such stark contrast to my own childhood experience that it is hard to write about even today. As punishment for some offense my father had committed, my grandfather made him squat down as a baseball catcher but did not allow him to use a glove! When I think of the thousands of pitches I threw to my dad, usually at his insistence, so that I could become a better pitcher—those pitches often hitting him in the shins and ankles—I know the pain must have returned him to cold, bitter days in his backyard, when fastballs from his drunk father caromed off his innocent, defenseless body.

When you stop the legacy of addiction and abuse in a family system, you take on generational pain that has been pushed aside, repressed, and evaded in the process. My father would sometimes have to leave our house to walk the 1.2 mile circle around our neighborhood block to avoid repeating similar discipline responses with his strong-willed, stubborn, and rebellious son. I am so grateful that Simon sacrificed his legs and redeemed his history for my heart and my future. Indeed, both our parents were system stoppers. All the generations after us owe them a debt of gratitude that can only be repaid in heaven.

My dad was also anti-establishment and anti-authority long before he became a part of the establishment and the authority of UC. His track record for doing his own thing and carving his own path were firmly rooted in his entrepreneurial father and now have bloomed through his three children. Simon did not like people telling him what to do, and if he did not respect the authority's intellect, work ethic, or passion, he could not and would not be under their direction. He told me many times that if I wanted to quit following directions from other people than I had better work hard enough and smart enough to be put in charge, become the leader, and make the decisions myself. "Andersons are made to lead, not to follow," he would tell me, knowing I had great leadership potential waiting to emerge despite (and sometimes because of) the anti-authority behavior.

One of the only positive communications my dad shared from his father was through the phrase, "Smile when you say that, Slim." It was a quote his grandfather told his father, who then used it with his two sons, and Simon used it with us. The phrase is meant as a communication warning, as a moment of pause and consideration before stubborn, strong-willed responses cross the line into disobedience and disrespect. Because a quick wit, a sarcastic tongue, and a strong will resonate through four generations of

Andersons, this line had ample opportunity for expression!

When Simon said this to Warren or me, it accompanied a mixture of pride and consternation. He wanted us to stand up for ourselves, to use our intelligence and communication skills to make a difference, to debate, argue, and even demand our point of view be considered. These, of course, were things he had willed himself to do since he did not have the privilege of fathering himself as he fathered us. Because of my propensity for popping off at the mouth, I heard this statement hundreds of times, and something about the way he said it and the story behind it curtailed my verbosity of the moment.

But there was something even stronger behind this phrase than a reminder of ultimate authority. There was the trace of the Anderson history, which like that of many Americans, includes the story of pioneers who risked everything to find a better place to live, a better country, a better life. I know this phrase brought back positive memories of my grandfather for my dad, memories of the music, memories of the family gift, memories of what could have been if what was taken away had not been so permanent and lasting. My father feared his father, but the respect was limited, and he spent most of his father years becoming the father his father could or would not be. Like every hardship Simon suffered, he chose to turn this into an opportunity for change, growth, development, and excellence. He chose to be a great father and knew that to do that, he was going to have to submit to the authority of God, the spirit and the structure of his wife, and the commitment to give us the upbringing he didn't receive.

Ephesians 6:4: *"Fathers, do not provoke your children to anger, but bring them up in the discipline and the instruction of the Lord."*

"Authority without wisdom is like a heavy axe without an edge, fitter to bruise than to polish."
— **Anne Bradstreet**

The Rhinelander Shorties Quartet, Rhinelander, WI 1948: Jack (Simon's brother), Simon, Herb Schauder, and John (Simon's father)

Simon Says:

Will you seek forgiveness or reconciliation with a family member?

>If yes, give yourself a time frame for the conversation.

_____

_____

Will you see a counselor about some of the family issues that have troubled you?

>If yes, give yourself a deadline for securing a session.

_____

_____

Will you apologize to your children for harsh or overly critical discipline?

> If yes, do it today.

Will you use the difficult parts of your past for inspiration and movement toward change?

> If yes, begin to shape a plan for a new perspective.

_____

_____

_____

_____

_____

Will you trust God's hand in your future and submit to his authority and his purposes?

> If yes, find an accountability partner to live with this purpose. Who could that same-gendered partner be? Ask them.

___

Otto (my soccer nickname), Seven Hills Middle School Vikings, 1980

Chapter 7
"Bravo!"
Encouragement and Belief

To hear "Bravo!" bellowed by my father was a great joy, one which superseded even accomplishing whatever it was we had just achieved. In my athletic career it was an addictive praise I longed to hear and strove to provoke from him. Simon loved basketball and baseball, and I was a strong enough player in both sports to have many opportunities to produce results that he understood, which often warranted a "Bravo!" Soccer, however, was another story, even though it was probably my best sport through middle school. If I played well but hadn't scored a goal, he would be bored and disappointed even when my coaches told him I had dictated the mid-field and controlled the flow of the game. Eventually, I gave up explaining the nuances of soccer and accepted the fact he wouldn't ever be a huge fan of the sport. Looking back, it's not a surprise I focused on baseball and basketball in high school and college.

One time in eighth grade, however, I scored four goals before halftime, prompting a "Bravo!" following the fourth goal. This is the only time I recall hearing "Bravo" from my dad for soccer—despite the 100-plus goals I scored in my youth and the handful of times I scored four or five goals in a game—and why I still remember almost every detail of the moment. I received a pass just outside of the 18' line, split two defenders by popping the ball over their feet off my trap, darted between them to retrieve the ball, and then poked it on the outside of my left foot to get

"Bravo!"

around the last defender, whom I jumped over as he tried a slide tackle. Then, without looking, I buried a one-touch, left-footed missile into the upper right-hand corner as the goalie stood frozen. As I returned to my center-mid position, I was shocked to hear my dad's distinctive call of affirmation and approval. "Bravo!" "Bravo!" Simon bellowed. I could have stopped playing the game and gone home. I had finally earned a "Bravo!" for soccer. We won the match 5-2, but we didn't score in the second half as our coach moved us to a defensive formation to protect our lead. On the way home, Simon noted the second half was really boring.

"Bravo!" by Simon in a private setting was usually followed by laughter and chortling that was similar to a Santa's "Ho, Ho, Ho." It was an exclamation point of joy in what his children, a performer, or his choir had just accomplished. The laughter often brought him to spontaneous tears and the need to dry his face with his hankie. In basketball, if I were putting on a show with my passing and dribbling, I could get four or five "Bravo!"s a game and maybe even make him change hankies. I cherished every one of those "Bravo!"s. Sometimes, I tried an even greater improvisational play in order to provoke a "Bravo!" from my father in the stands.

"Bravo!" is a phrase that originated in Italy and was used most frequently in theater and concert, particularly opera, performances. The audience would stand up and shout "Bravo!" for a performance that had fulfilled or exceeded expectations. Today we use it more individually to celebrate somebody's success by communicating our happiness for them on a job well done. Simon believed in encouragement, and though he demanded excellence from his children, students, and choirs, when we met his expectations, he would gladly communicate encouragement and positivity. This exuberance in praise didn't mean he wouldn't criticize or challenge those under his guidance and leadership. On the contrary, he could be very sharp and sting you with his critiques, but it was always out of a desire for you to maximize your full potential. And it wasn't usually an imperfect result that flustered him the most. It was if your heart was clearly not in it or the commitment was missing. Some people are more talented and naturally gifted than others. Simon understood that. But the playing field is equal when it comes to energy, effort, and work ethic, and that is what Simon most wanted to see.

It really comes down to belief: what we believe about God, what we believe about self, and what we believe about community. Even though Simon had a difficult time with all three categories in his childhood and youth, he was determined to find out what he could accomplish as an adult when he started choosing to believe in the goodness of God, marriage, family, self, and community. He chose not to use his own father's acidic negativity as an excuse to poison us with the same. He chose to believe in us even when we failed. For example, almost every time we left the office of a principal together—almost a monthly occurrence with me for a few years—and after I had received a stern lecture and the consequences for my inappropriate behavior or communication, he would remind me of my strengths and point me toward my future. "Elliott," he would say on the walk to the station wagon as my head was bowed and my feet dragged behind his, "despite your best efforts to undermine your future, people really like you. When you harness your energy and learn some self-discipline, you will be a fantastic leader." His belief in our potential was so strong that at times it seemed as if he was prophetic. I watched his students address him publicly as a beacon of hope and a pillar of strength—someone who had inspired them to believe in themselves, someone who had shaped their careers and relationships. All three of Simon's teaching children have aspired to do the same.

Positive reinforcement is a critical tool in shaping behavior and effort. It goes hand in hand with belief.

"Bravo!"

If children do not receive positive verbal and non-verbal reinforcement from their parents, teachers, and family, they will have a very difficult time believing in themselves, even if they are supremely talented and gifted. But the same is true for adults. We all need appreciation and affirmation in our lives, and the simplest way to achieve this is to encourage each other regularly. Too often we are worried about someone not noticing our strengths and abilities, and in our self-absorption we miss wonderful opportunities to encourage others. The less we focus on self and the more we focus on others, the easier true, meaningful encouragement becomes. I don't know where you need a "Bravo!" in your life, but I know if Simon were around to observe your daily activities, he would find a way to encourage you and believe in you and your future.

> **1 Thessalonians 5:14**, *"And we urge you, brothers, admonish the idle, encourage the fainthearted, help the weak, be patient with them all."*

"It's what you choose to believe that makes you the person you are." — **Karen Marie Moning**

Receiving the University of Cincinnati Faculty Recognition Award in support of the educational advancement of student-athletes during Simon's 41-year tenure 1963-2004.

"Bravo!"

Simon Says:

Where do you need to be encouraged right now?

_____

_____

_____

Do you lack belief in yourself regarding this issue?

     Yes   No

If yes, who can encourage you to overcome or work through this issue?

_____

_____

_____

Who needs your belief to encourage them right now?

_____

_____

_____

How can you show them this encouragement?

_____

_____

_____

Will you make encouraging and positive communication a consistent pattern in your life?

"Bravo!"

Will you believe in the goodness of yourself and believe in the goodness of others?

List 5 positive things you believe about yourself.

1. _____

2. _____

3. _____

4. _____

5. _____

Ascension Lutheran Church Choir, 2001

Chapter 8
"In the House *of the Lord"*
Faith and Family

Most of us get the foundation of our faith passed onto us from our family. Whether we stay with that faith or not, we are working off of, against, or away from that modeling. Grandpa John, Simon's father, was not a man prone to dependency on anybody or anything outside of music and alcohol, God notwithstanding. The family attended a Lutheran church in Rhinelander, but there was not much interaction, community, or life-giving experience that stabilized or encouraged his family or a personal faith.

And yet, when my father was looking for a wife after his stint in the Army, he instinctively and intentionally found a devout and dedicated Christian woman. He needed Nancy's faith for himself, and he also wanted his children to have a faith foundation in God—and to be directed in this faith through the family—something he had not received. Though my father believed in God and gave of his time, talents, and treasures to the Church, my mother was always the bedrock of our Christian faith. Our father was the head of the family in decisions, provision, protection, and spirit, but our mother was the spiritual leader.

Therefore, just like the other areas in my mother's life, consistent commitment, engagement, and service in the Church was never a question; it was a part of the fabric of our lives. Worship services, pot-luck dinners, youth groups, Bible studies, prayer meetings, retreats,

"In the House of the Lord"

athletic leagues, mission trips, and summer camps were all woven into our family dynamic. Because of Simon's random and hyper nature, it made sense to him that if he were going to be at Church every week, then he might as well lead the music ministry and use his gifts for the Lord and make some extra income for the family at the same time. So, for almost 50 years, he was the music minister at four different churches.

His longest tenure was at 9th Street Baptist Church in downtown Cincinnati. His service there culminated with our childhood, and 9th Street was also the church with the doctrine and polity that matched closest to my mother's home church and her heart. All of us had great friends at 9th Street, and our music ministry careers were initiated there, as were dating relationships and an understanding the importance of service. We also were blessed through dedicated and selfless Sunday school teachers and youth group leaders and the parents and families of our friends. It was a great home church in which to learn about God and experience a community of faith.

As a child, on occasion (or almost every week) I would have a difficult time containing my energy and spirit in the Church structure. Being at church from 8:00 a.m. to 12:00 p.m. every Sunday morning, despite the fun I had with my friends, was a long time to behave, sit still, and stay out of trouble. Consequently, there were wheelchair races, pew-surfing contests (crawling underneath the pew seats from the front to the back of the auditorium), and snack-stealing or pencil-flicking shenanigans (placing the small pew pencils in the middle of the hymnal and flicking them a great distance, one time, up and over the pastor's head during the service), and just general, mostly innocent, mayhem.

Inevitably, after church, and by the time we all loaded up in the station wagon to go out to eat at Frisch's, I had instigated some type of fracas with my siblings.

Often, Simon would have me ride up in the front seat (which, of course, I loved), to squelch the misbehavior, but if Warren or Karin wanted to see me in trouble, it did not take much to enrage my temper or chaotic responses with a subtle look or a wry comment. If the fighting and arguing persisted beyond Simon's initial thwarting, then a theological mandate from on high was soon to follow, right about the time we hit the Hopple St. exit.

"We have just worshiped in the house of the Lord," Dad would bellow, in full Corbett Auditorium lecture voice. "Could you please act as if it made a difference?" Several more sentences of similar persuasion were usually offered, but the point had been made. If you won't behave or quit fooling around on my behalf, you should do it for the Lord. Thus, the ultimate trump card of authority had been used. And most of the time, the house of the Lord sermonette would subdue the tide of trouble for at least five minutes or until we made it into the restaurant, whichever came first. (There, normally, the chaos would begin all over again, until I was ordered to finish my meal in the car with the Reds or Bengals game on the radio for my company.)

This ultimate authority of the Lord is the key to our family's peace and resilience in the faith. God is the ultimate authority and ruler of life. He is Sovereign. He reigns supreme forever and ever, amen. We have had our share of suffering and sorrows, including obviously, watching Simon waste away with vascular dementia, but our faith in God, our eternity in heaven, and our experience depending upon the Lord and each other for comfort and care remains. It is true. It is real. And we are a testimony to the life, death, and resurrection of Jesus Christ. Simon was not outwardly evangelistic with his relationships, but his commitment to faith and family was legitimate, and his favorite tactic for faith engagement was to simply invite you to sing in his choir. He would let the words of the hymn, anthem, or cantata do the work of the Spirit in your heart. He just brought you into God's house and let the Lord and the Church do the rest.

Simon would have never predicted his pencil-flicking son would end up an ordained pastor, and he was troubled, at first, when I told him of my calling. Similar to how he responded to Karin's year of mission work in Philadelphia, there were questions to be answered, but he always came around to support and respect—not to mention financially invest in—our convictions. By the time I finished college, he had sponsored and endowed multiple summers of music ministry across the Midwest with his children and our college friends performing contemporary Christian music concerts. We would load up three of his station wagons and away we went.

This prodigal took some time to submit to the ultimate authority, and pretty much any authority outside of athletic coaches for the first 20 years of my life, but the calling on all of our lives to live for the Kingdom of God is sincere and rooted in the faith Simon and Nancy instilled in us. They also participated in the faith-root watering of hundreds of University of Cincinnati students, Seven Hills Schools students, Friars Club athletes, Clifton Hills Avenue neighborhood families, and, of course, community members in the churches where Simon and Nancy ministered together. Every church that received my father as musical leader received my mother as a lead soprano, church librarian, Sunday school teacher, and pie-baker, as well. They were a great team and enjoyed contributing to a church body together.

And just as Simon was eclectic with his musical taste and appreciation, he was eclectic in his faith, serving in four well-known branches of American Protestant churches: Walnut Hills-Avondale United Methodist Church; 9th Street Baptist Church, Maderia Presbyterian Church, and Ascension Lutheran Church. And whether it was a Methodist, Baptist, Presbyterian, or Lutheran service didn't much matter to Simon, though I think he was most comfortable at Ascension with the liturgy of his youth. He knew his job was to usher the people into the house of the Lord through the music—his heart song, his most intimate form of worship. And in the latter years of his life, he loved to attend Crossroads Community Church, the popular megachurch, with all the passion, energy, and excellence they exuded in the name of Christ, especially in their music.

So, what about your faith? Have you spent time considering your place in eternity? Your relationship with God? What you believe about Jesus? In true Simon fashion, with some authoritative professorial wit attached, he would highly encourage you to take the time to find out for yourself what is true about Christianity. Simon was an insatiable researcher, and he would challenge you to research for yourself the claims of the Bible to discover why he followed my mother's lead and chose a faith in Jesus Christ as His

Lord and Savior and why he raised his family to live in the same manner.

Genesis 28:16-17: *"Surely the Lord in in this place, and I did not know it. How awesome is this place! This is none other than the house of the Lord, and this is the gate of Heaven."*

"Imagine yourself as a living house. God comes in to rebuild that house. You thought you were being made into a decent little cottage, but God is building a palace. He intends to come and live in it Himself."
— C.S. Lewis

Nancy and Simon and their six grandchildren: Amie, Eliah, Alivia (with Grandma), Jacob, Paige (with Grandpa), and Austin, 2003

Simon Says:

<u>Books on Christianity the Anderson family recommends for research</u>

Timothy Keller	*The Reason for God*
C.S. Lewis	*Mere Christianity*
Max Lucado	*God Came Near*
Josh McDowell	*Evidence that Demands a Verdict*
Lee Strobel	*The Case for Christ*
Chuck Swindoll	*Jesus: The Greatest Life of All*
N.T. Wright	*Simply Christian*

Do you have a faith foundation passed down from your family?   Yes   No

Are you secure in your faith in Christ as your Savior?

Yes   No

If yes, return to the roots of your faith and the commitment of your soul.

If no, ask the Lord to reveal Himself to you, and

we believe that He will do so.

If no, will you be willing to investigate the life of Jesus Christ for yourself?

Would you like to ask Jesus to be your Lord and Savior now?

"In the House of the Lord"

If yes, consider a prayer like this:

"Dear Lord, I need you in my life and ask for you to forgive me for my sins. Please come into my heart and give me your life, love, peace, and joy. Heal my heart and soul from the stain of sin and allow me to be used for your glory. I want to change my relationships to reflect your grace and truth. I want to change my perspective to represent your love for community and the church. I want to be used by you for your Kingdom to bring joy and hope to the world. Amen."

New Year's Eve at the Deupree House, 1988

Chapter 9
"Rucka Chucka, Rucka Chucka"
Rhythm and Responsibility

Playing dance jobs with my dad was intimidating. He was the Music Man of Cincinnati and we were his children. We had to be very good musicians also. There wasn't really a choice. Warren had the strongest musical abilities and was the oldest son, so the pressure was greatest on him, but my dad had high expectations for all of us—especially with music. He expected Warren and me to play jazz like it was our primary musical genre, as if we had grown up listening to Benny Goodman and Tommy Dorsey. He wanted Karin to sing like Rosemary Clooney or Doris Day. My mother felt it, too, as she was the lead soprano soloist in whatever choir they were in together, not easy when your husband is the director.

And it didn't matter if we were playing dinner music at the Millcroft Inn or dance music for a huge reception at the Hyatt; Simon played every dance job the same—all out—and with everything he had. "It is my responsibility," he would tell us, "to play my absolute best with full energy and passion every time I play." Therefore, we were to do the same. "We are there for the people," he'd say. "They are paying us to entertain them, and that is what we are going to do!" Simon was known around Cincinnati as a master educator, performer, and entertainer, and he did not ever want to jeopardize that. That meant that we couldn't jeopardize it, either.

"Rucka Chucka, Rucka Chucka"

As a young drummer, I often played more softly and slowly than he wanted, and he would let me know about it. "Elliott, you have to lay the foundation." "Elliott, you have to drive the song." "Elliott, you are behind." "Elliott, play like you mean it." And eventually, when I started to lay down the right groove, he would turn to me with a smile on his face, a twinkle in his eye, and using his arm like a railroad wheel with his fist accentuating the tempo he'd say, "Rucka chucka, rucka chucka."

No one knows what "Rucka chucka, rucka chucka" means (he never explained it to us), but I believe the four hard sounds—*ruh, kuh, chuh, kuh*"—are the four 16th notes in a measure of 4/4 time, with the *ch* of the *chucka* representing the snare sound. Whatever it meant, make no mistake, he knew what he wanted the drums to sound like, and he knew what he wanted his musicians to do: play with passion, heart, and rhythm. It sometimes took a set or two, but whenever he finally turned to me and said, "Rucka chucka, rucka chucka," it meant he was pleased with my playing and energy, and he wanted me to lock in right there for the rest of the night.

Rhythm was a big deal to Simon. It was a big deal to his music and to his life. His own rhythm was full throttle, high-octane passion and energy. His capacity for work was enormous, and his ability to take on huge responsibilities and direct major musical operations on top of the classes he taught was remarkable. Rhythm to Simon was about tempo and style. He was random. He was spontaneous, but he was also organized and disciplined. Therefore, within a typical day Simon would usually get done what he wanted to get done, but the tasks and duties came with great variations in timing and order. And if he decided to run an errand in the middle of a lecture preparation, so be it, and off he went. Even if he had to go that same direction an hour later, he allowed his natural rhythm to lead him. His effectiveness was not always based on efficiency, and he gave himself permission to take a nap, investigate a research diversion, watch five minutes of the NBA Game of the Week with me, discuss a composition with Warren, or talk to Karin and her friends—but then it was back to the grind.

Because his unique rhythms were successful for him, he was adamant that you followed your natural rhythms, as well. Nancy, for example, is extremely organized, linear, and concrete. Everything she does has order and purpose, and she follows those routines religiously and without consideration of another way. Needless to say, this was the exact opposite of my father, but within their marriage and family they allowed each of the two individual styles to have meaning, importance, and a place. This allowed their children to benefit from both styles rather than having to submit or align to just one or the other.

Warren is an introverted, structured night owl who enjoys spicy foods, southern gospel music, and Agatha Christie books. He is a natural leader with natural direction and inspires people like Simon did. He has worked at Judson University for over 30 years and will likely retire from there, as well. I am an extroverted, hyper, morning person who keeps a clean room, listens to rap, and loves sports. My leadership is based on relational community and creating a culture. I have had six different careers already, and I am sure there are a few more left. Karin likes heavy metal and horror movies, and she is an extroverted, social machine as a gifted hostess and relational conduit. She leads through deep connection, inspired teaching, and genuine empathy for everybody.

The main point is that each of us was free to live within these rhythms and styles as long as the results were excellent and the responsibilities were done. If they weren't, then you would usually have to comply with my mom's order because it was more consistent and dependable for details and instant accountability. But that was just for the temporary requirement; then it was back to how God had wired you and how you unlocked your passion and fully engaged spirit.

To have the freedom to be yourself within a family system is a tremendous blessing. And since Simon hated the status quo, he even encouraged you to think and behave outside of the box and against the grain. But again, I want to reinforce that the responsibilities had to be fulfilled within your personal rhythms and style. In fact, Simon believed you had a responsibility to yourself within the responsibilities to your employer and community to live within your rhythms. And he talked about tempo and style in everything you did—sports, music, academics, art, reading, eating, and performing.

In order to live in this manner, you have to know yourself well enough to be yourself. If your responsibilities do not allow you to live within your rhythms, then he encouraged you to fulfill what you had committed to and then move on to something different. Find people and employment that appreciate, affirm, and encourage you to be who you are, and you will be successful and satisfied . . . and have fun while you are at it. Anything outside of that and you are just collecting a paycheck or being complacent in your relationships. Unacceptable! Rucka chucka, rucka chucka!

Psalm 139:14: *"I praise you because I am fearfully and wonderfully made."*

"It's not your responsibility to have the life that others want for you." — **Colin Wright**

Aunt Patty (Simon's older sister), 50th Anniversary Party, Rhinelander, WI, 1996

"Rucka Chucka, Rucka Chucka"

Simon Says:

Do you know your natural rhythms?

    Introvert or Extravert?

    Morning Person or Night Person?

    Structured or Random?

    Clean or Messy?

    Hyper or Reserved?

    Verbal Processor or Mental Processor?

    Love of Big Groups or Small Groups?

Do your responsibilities allow you to live in your natural rhythms?

    With your parents?

    With your siblings?

    With your spouse?

    With your children?

    With your work?

    With your church?

    With your community?

Write about your natural rhythms.
Do your loved ones know what these are?
They need to.

"Rucka Chucka, Rucka Chucka"

Expecting Warren, 1963 Apartment in Cincinnati

Chapter 10
"Glad to Be Here"
Joy and Passion

Unlike the other iconic phrases Simon intentionally communicated frequently to those under his authority or instruction, he only uttered "Glad to be here" socially and in neutral relational circumstances. I first recall hearing the phrase in a moment when Simon was caught off guard socially, something that rarely occurred since his popularity in the city led to consistent recognition and affirmation of his teaching and performances. A preadolescent youth at the time,

I didn't understand what these social connections cost my private and introverted father in space and energy, but the small measure of his Cincinnati fame was obviously worth the exchange and his need for relational recovery. When time allowed or necessity required, he'd bury himself in his office at home or at U.C., researching, reading, listening, writing, or composing. This professional preparation also afforded him the isolation he needed to refuel, so, when demanded of him, he could socialize outside of his relational comfortability.

Therefore, when we were in public, Dr. Anderson was always ready for a quick conversation or connection with colleagues, choir members, social acquaintances, or former students. He expected them. He looked for them. He mentally prepared for them. We knew these encounters fed his ego, but we also watched it feed the masses. Simon understood human nature and the universal need to be identified and remembered with positivity and enthusiasm by those within our community. That is why the phrase "Glad to be here" made the Top Ten *Simon Says* list, not for its place in our day-to-day upbringing but for its summative ideology of Simon's ethos in life. Simon believed joy must be your mark and passion must ooze from your pores. When you genuinely enjoy your marriage, family, friends, work, church, and community, your attitude, energy, influence, and impact in those relational and social endeavors will be positive and possibly even profound. This can be accomplished no matter what your background and what you've overcome, with any and all personalities and temperaments. It's a matter of daily perspective so beautifully shared in Psalm 118:24: *"This is the day which the Lord has made; let us rejoice and be glad in it."*

The first time we heard Simon utter this phrase took place on a Sunday afternoon in the late 1970's. It was after church and after one of my soccer games, which meant we had infringed on Simon's Sunday routine of church, Frisch's Big Boy, a nap, and church again. Therefore, Simon's quota for social and relational connection had already been reached, with the evening service still to orchestrate. Furthermore, we were all super hungry and crabby and had settled on a restaurant we hardly ever chose, a Ponderosa that was located on Ridge Road near Madison Road I assume Simon made this choice without family consensus because he wanted a steak (steak was his economic comfort food for his worn-out soul; it reminded him how far he had come out of poverty) and because he was still hours away from enjoying a vodka and orange juice, some jazz, and some time alone.

We ordered our food and found our table, but, right before Simon sat down, a man he knew from one of his many community-relations efforts approached assertively, startling our tired and famished dad. "Simon," the man said with great enthusiasm and energy, something my father usually admired and preferred in social connection, before babbling on for several minutes and beyond the boundaries of social graces, without pausing or allowing any reciprocal communication from my now slightly irritated father. The man ended his monologue of self-importance with "So glad to see you," to which Simon retorted, "Glad to be here."

As with most intellectual men, Simon had a sharp wit which occasionally included an acidic and sarcastic tongue. We usually only heard this communicated publicly when members of the service industry did not serve, members of the education community did not educate, or a member of the Cincinnati Police felt Simon had earned a speeding or parking ticket. Simon felt a responsibility to redirect their erroneous mentality with a biting assessment of their failure to fulfill their job descriptions. They were often very funny comments, even when, as a future counselor, I felt empathy for the recipients. In this particular scenario, however, I don't know if he was intentionally funny, sarcastic, dismissive, or, frankly, tired, hungry, and annoyed that a quick response using the man's own words just spontaneously emerged from his lips. No matter what the motivation behind Simon's instinctive verbal response, the man left the restaurant quickly and our family burst into laughter. We have replayed the humorous interruption for 40 years.

Despite his family's response to this random reply, Simon continued to use the phrase in social situations and gatherings as long as he lived. I mostly heard it shared at large events where Simon would be a tad uncomfortable—weddings, funerals, and parties where he didn't have an authoritative or performance role. People were genuinely glad to see Dr. Anderson. He was charismatic in energy, spirit, and verbosity. He loved to hear people share about their passions the way he shared about music. It didn't matter if he had absolutely no interest in the topic or theme. If you had some serious joy concerning your area of interest or study or your career, he loved to hear about it. But if you were a world-renowned expert who communicated with zero passion and little joy, he would tune out in seconds. Though Simon despised small talk and often dreaded large social gatherings, he was truly glad to be there if it served a positive purpose and provided anyone encouragement in life. How many times have we bemoaned a large social event we needed to attend only to have a wonderful time once we succumbed to the commitment and the connection with the people?

Glad to be here. Glad to be alive. Glad to take part in the life and love of family and community. Glad to have a job. Glad to have our health. How important it is to have a perspective of gladness and appreciation in life because we know things rarely go as planned. We are interrupted by well-meaning and well-intended family and friends. We are persecuted and mistreated by those who don't like us and oppose us, or when we stand in their way. Our company lays us off despite our dedication, loyalty, and spotless record. Our spouse leaves us for another love even though we were faithful, gracious and loving. Our children rebel. Our neighbor moves. Our pastor leaves. How will we respond to these interruptions? Can you be glad to be there, wherever there is?

We recognize now more than ever that life is fragile. Change and crisis can occur from every direction and in any manner. Despite the unpredictability and inconsistency of our world right now, we always have a choice. We always have an opportunity. We can determine how we will respond—maybe not immediately, as our mind, heart, and body will think, emote, and viscerally react to the stimuli and situations around us, but, in time, we will be able to process and consciously choose how we will respond. Will we see the glass as empty, half-empty, half-full, or all the way full? Will we allow the circumstances around us to create our environmental and cultural conditions, or will we determine the culture of our community through our relational and social communication?

Simon overcame poverty, abuse, insecurity, inferiority, height issues, hair issues, teeth issues, the Army, and even vascular dementia. He lived a life of joy and passion, peace and prosperity, commitment and conviction, family and faith. Throughout his 85 years he learned how to be joyful wherever he was, even in the nursing home where he spent his last days, shuffling and organizing papers at the main desk and charming the nurses with his eyes and his smile. It was brutally difficult to watch a brilliant man lose his intellect, his comprehension, his ability to communicate, and his basic functioning over a slow, steady decline during his last five years. But we were amazed at his countenance and presence, for even when he no longer understood the world around him, his spirit and soul stayed the same. He died how he lived. There was joy in his heart. There was passion in his spirit. There was still piano strength in his hands. There was life and love in his eyes until the Lord called him home. He was glad to be here, and now he is glad to be in Heaven. How will you live the rest of your days on earth? Will you join Simon in joy and passion? Will you be glad to be here?

Psalm 100:1: *"Shout joyfully to the Lord, all the earth. Serve the Lord with gladness; come before Him with joyful singing."*

"We must act out passion before we feel it."
— **Jean-Paul Sartre**

Joseph-Beth Booksellers, Simon's last regular gig in the early 2000's

"Glad to Be Here"

Simon Says:

Where do you find the most joy and passion?

_____

_____

_____

Where can you find more joy and more passion and with what people or community?

_____

_____

_____

What robs you of joy in your life?

_____

_____

_____

How can you remove this obstacle or issue or at least change your attitude or perspective?

_____

_____

_____

List three things you are really passionate about.

1._____

2._____

3._____

Are you engaged in these passions regularly?

    If not, find a way to do so.

Are these passions bringing you and others joy?

    If yes, continue them and share them.

    If no, it may be time to find more passions or to change patterns within these passions

Practicing in the basement, 1980

About the Author

Elliott J. Anderson is Pastor to Staff and Faculty and Assistant Professor of Psychology at Judson University. Previous roles at Judson include Director of the Wellness Center, Vice President for Student Life, Dean of Students, Resident Director, and Head Coach of both Men's Basketball and Baseball. Elliott's MA is in Counseling Psychology from Trinity Evangelical Divinity School, and he is ordained through the Southern Baptist denomination. He was Senior Pastor at Elgin Evangelical Free Church and has been a teaching pastor at two other Elgin Baptist churches. He has also been a Crisis Family Therapist and owned multiple home service businesses. Elliott has been married to Angie for over thirty years. They have four children and also are licensed foster parents. *Answers in Abundance* was his first published book telling the story of their journey through ten years of infertility, adoption, and biological births. His romance novel, *It's About Time*, will also be published this Christmas season.

4 Anderson Professors

For More Information

The legacy of *Simon Says* lives on in various incarnations. For more of his wit and wisdom or that which he passed on to his children, consider the following resources:

Simon's two music textbooks, *The Musical Imperative* and *Pop Music, U.S.A.*, can be obtained through Clifton Hills Press, Inc.: cliftonhillspress.com.

Warren writes a weekly blog at emmausroadworshipers.com (to which anyone can subscribe) and a weekly encouragement e-mail. Contact him at wanderson@judsonu.edu for information.

In addition to *Simon Says*, Elliott has written *Answers in Abundance*, a memoir of the adoption of twin boys and subsequent birth of two daughters, all in a three-year span. It is available through Amazon. He can be reached at elliott.anderson@judsonu.edu.

Karin writes, podcasts, and speaks, nationally and internationally, in both academic and pop-psych arenas, under the umbrella of her platform, *Love & Life*. Information on *Single is the New Black: Don't Wear White 'til it's Right* (her book), *Love & Life with Dr. Karin* (her podcast), and speaking engagements, can be accessed at loveandlifemedia.com.

www.ingramcontent.com/pod-product-compliance
Lightning Source LLC
LaVergne TN
LVHW051603070426
835507LV00021B/2746